CLASSIFYING ANIMALS

Amphibians

Sarah Wilkes

HODDER
Wayland

An imprint of Hodder Children's Books

CLASSIFYING ANIMALS

Titles in this series:

Amphibians Birds Fish Insects Mammals Reptiles

For more information on this series and other Hodder Wayland titles, go to www.hodderwayland.co.uk

Conceived and produced for Hodder Wayland by

Nutshell
MEDIA

www.nutshellmedialtd.co.uk

Consultant: Jane Mainwaring, Natural History Museum
Editor: Polly Goodman
Designer: Tim Mayer
Illustrator: Jackie Harland
Picture research: Morgan Interactive Ltd and Victoria Coombs

Published in Great Britain in 2005 by Hodder Wayland, an imprint of Hodder Children's Books.

British Library Cataloguing in Publication Data
Wilkes, Sarah, 1964–
Amphibians. – (Classifying animals)
1. Amphibians – Classification – Juvenile literature
I. Title
597.8'012

ISBN 0 7502 4750 9

Cover photograph: red-eyed tree frog
Title page (clockwise from top left): Madagascan mandella; European toad; red-eyed tree frog; male and female Alpine newts.
Chapter openers (from top to bottom): the skin of a horned frog, common frog spawn, the skin of a broad-mouth frog, a golden poison arrow frog and a European toad.

Picture acknowledgements
Corbis cover; **Ecoscene** 4 (Clive Druett), 14 bottom (Paul Franklin), 16 (Reinhard Dirscheri), 28, 29, 30 (Robert Pickett), 35 (Anthony Cooper), 42 (Wayne Lawler); **naturepl.com** 6 (Morley Read), 8 (Hans Christoph Kappel), 9, 10 (Barry Mansell), 11 (Doug Wechsler), 12 (John Cancalosi), 13 (Doug Wechsler), 14 top, 15 (Fabio Liverani), 17 (Pete Oxford), 18 (Mark Payne-Gill), 19 (Marcelo rocha/John Downer Pr), 20 (Barry Mansell), 21 (Hans Christoph Kappel), 22 (David Welling), 23 (Barry Mansell), 24,. 25 (Pete Oxford), 26 (Barry Mansell), 27 (Pete Oxford), 31 (Fabio Liverani), 32 (Ingo Arndt), 33 (Phil Savoie), 34 (Bruce Davidson), 36 (Tony Phelps), 37 (David Shale), 38 (Pete Oxford), 39 Tim MacMillan/John Downer Pr), 40 (Claudio Velasquez), 41 (Pete Oxford), 43 (George McCarthy); **NHPA** 7 (Daniel Heuclin).

Printed and bound in China.

Hodder Children's Books
A division of Hodder Headline Limited
338 Euston Road, London NW1 3BH

CONTENTS

WHAT ARE AMPHIBIANS?

AMPHIBIANS ARE ANIMALS THAT CAN LIVE BOTH ON LAND and in water – the name 'amphibian' comes from the Greek word *amphibios,* meaning 'double life'. There are about 5,400 species of amphibians, including frogs, toads, newts, salamanders, and caecilians.

Amphibians are a class of vertebrates. All vertebrates have a vertebral column, which is a series of small bones that run down their back to provide support. There are seven other classes of vertebrates, including mammals, birds and reptiles.

Amphibian features

All amphibians share certain features by which they can be identified. They breathe through their moist skin as well as through their lungs. They have a long and often sticky tongue, and ears marked by an eardrum, but not external ear flaps like mammals. Most species smell using an area of nerve endings in the roof of their mouth, called the Jacobson's organ. Most amphibians have four limbs, with four digits on the front limbs and five digits on the hind limbs. All amphibians are ectothermic, or cold-blooded. This means that they rely on heat from their environment to keep their body warm and their body temperature fluctuates with the temperature of their surroundings.

The common frog (*Rana temporaria*) is a typical amphibian, with its moist skin and four limbs.

4

CLASSIFICATION

About 2 million different organisms have been identified and sorted into groups, in a process called classification. Biologists look at the similarities and differences between organisms, and group together those with shared characteristics. The largest grouping is the kingdom, for example the animal kingdom. Each kingdom is divided into smaller groups, called phyla (singular: phylum). Each phylum is divided into classes, which are divided into orders, then families, genera (singular: genus), and finally species. A species is a single type of organism with unique features that are different from all other organisms, for example a marbled salamander. Only members of the same species can reproduce with each other and produce fertile offspring.

The classification of the marbled salamander (*Ambystoma opacum*) is shown on the right.

KINGDOM: Animal
|
PHYLUM: Chordata
|
CLASS: Amphibia
|
ORDER: Caudata
|
FAMILY: Ambystomatidae
|
GENUS: Ambystoma
|
SPECIES: *opacum* (marbled salamander)

One way of remembering the order of the different groups is to learn this phrase:
'**K**ings **P**lay **C**hess **O**n **F**ridays **G**enerally **S**peaking'.

Life cycle

All amphibians go through a series of physical changes called metamorphosis. Most species lay eggs that hatch into larvae. The larvae go through a number of physical changes to become adults. Frogs lay eggs that hatch into larvae called tadpoles, which live in water and slowly change into small frogs. Most amphibians return to water to breed.

Amphibians are divided into three orders: caecilians (Gymnophiona), tailed amphibians (Caudata), and frogs and toads (Anura). This book looks at the orders and the families within them, examining their characteristics and the way each group is adapted to its environment. It is not possible to cover all the amphibian families in this book. However, there is a complete list of the families on page 44.

FROG LIFE CYCLE

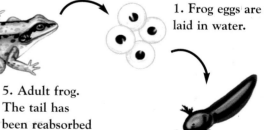

1. Frog eggs are laid in water.

2. Eggs hatch into tadpoles, which breathe using gills.

3. The tadpoles grow hind legs at 8 weeks and front legs at 12 weeks.

4. Froglet. The almost mature frog still has some of its tail but uses its lungs to breathe.

5. Adult frog. The tail has been reabsorbed by the body.

CAECILIANS (GYMNOPHIONA)

CAECILIANS ARE STRANGE, WORM-LIKE AMPHIBIANS that look nothing like frogs or toads. They are found in tropical parts of South America, Africa and Southeast Asia.

Shared features

There are 176 species of caecilians, divided into six families. They range in size from about 7–150 cm (3–60 in). All caecilians have a long body and no legs. Their tail is either tiny or virtually non-existent. Their skeleton lacks a pectoral (shoulders) or pelvic (hips) girdle. Their skull is massive and their eyes are tiny. Externally, they have a segmented appearance like a worm. Usually their skin is moist and smooth, although a few caecilians have some scales. Most caecilians have a single lung, although one species, called *Typhlonectes eiselti*, has no lungs. This species obtains all the oxygen it requires through its skin and mouth.

Underground living

Caecilians spend much of their life underground. They use their heavy head to push through the soil in search of worms, insects and other food, and to make burrows. They move forwards using muscular contractions and by pressing against the ground.

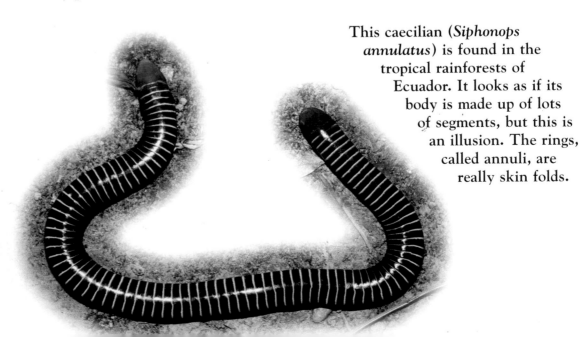

This caecilian (*Siphonops annulatus*) is found in the tropical rainforests of Ecuador. It looks as if its body is made up of lots of segments, but this is an illusion. The rings, called annuli, are really skin folds.

Caecilians have many needle-sharp teeth, which they use to catch and hold their prey. This caecilian is eating a worm. Caecilians also prey on termites, beetles, molluscs, small snakes, frogs and lizards. They swallow their prey whole.

Caecilians use a sensitive tentacle near their mouth to help find prey. The tentacle is retractable, so it can be pulled in while burrowing. Caecilians hunt their prey by creeping up on it. They have two rows of small, sharp teeth on their upper jaw and either one or two rows on the lower jaw, which they use to grip and crush prey. Some caecilians produce a toxic secretion from their skin to defend themselves from predators.

Life cycle

All caecilians reproduce by internal fertilization, where the male clasps the female and deposits his sperm inside her. The fertilized eggs develop in one of three ways. In some species, the eggs are laid in burrows near streams and hatch into larvae with gills. The larvae wiggle into the water where they go through metamorphosis, gradually changing into adult caecilians that will live on land. In some egg-laying species, the larvae go through metamorphosis while still in the egg and break out as miniature adults. Often, these eggs are guarded by the female. The third type of life cycle involves live bearers – species that give birth to live offspring. The eggs stay inside the body of the female for nine to eleven months, and hatch into larvae inside her. The larvae feed on a milk-like secretion produced by the female before they are born as tiny adults.

KEY CHARACTERISTICS
GYMNOPHIONA

- **Long body, no limbs and virtually no tail.**
- **Heavy skull and small eyes.**
- **Segmented appearance.**

TAILED AMPHIBIANS (CAUDATA)

TAILED AMPHIBIANS MAKE UP THE SECOND-LARGEST amphibian order. The order Caudata contains 470 species of sirens, salamanders and newts, that are found all over the world apart from Australia and Antarctica.

The order Caudata is divided into three superfamilies: sirens (Sirenoidea), giant salamanders (Cryptobranchoidea), and salamanders and newts (Salamandroidea). The different superfamilies are identified by the position of various bones in their skull. The adults range in size from a few centimetres to just under 2 m (6.5 ft).

Caudata features

Tailed amphibians are easily distinguished from other amphibians because the larvae, juveniles and adults all have a tail. The tail is particularly long in the adults. Most adults have two pairs of legs of similar size, which extend at right angles from their body. The exception is the siren, which lacks any hind limbs. The larvae have teeth on both their upper and lower jaw, as well as gill slits and external gills.

The European fire salamander (*Salamandra salamandra*) is a relatively large salamander, ranging in size from about 12–30 cm (5–12 in) long. It has a double line of poison glands running along its back and more poison glands along both sides of its body.

Reproduction

Sirens and giant salamanders are ancient amphibians and still fertilize their eggs in the water. This is called external fertilization. The female releases eggs, which are fertilized by the male sperm in the water. Salamanders and newts practise internal fertilization.

Habitat

Some tailed amphibians are terrestrial, living most of their life on land, while others are aquatic and spend their entire lives in water. Some terrestrial amphibians return to water to breed, while others lay their eggs on land. Most terrestrial species live on the forest floor. They hide under rocks or logs in the daytime and emerge at night to feed. Aquatic species live on the bottoms of streams or ponds, often under stones.

Food

Tailed amphibians are carnivorous animals and they hunt a range of invertebrates, such as worms and insects. Often they use their long tongue to catch prey. Their well-developed tails are ideal for powering swimming.

The Alabama waterdog (*Necturus alabamensis*) is a medium-sized salamander measuring 15–22 cm (6–9 in) long, with well-developed legs and four digits on both front and back feet. The adults retain their external gills and have fins.

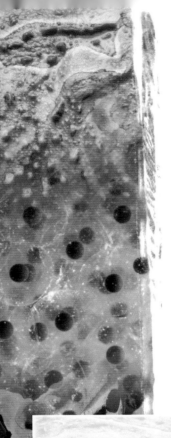

SIRENS (SIRENOIDEA)

SIRENS ARE EEL-LIKE SALAMANDERS THAT LIVE IN WATER. There are just four species of sirens, found in the south-eastern parts of the USA and in north-east Mexico.

Siren features

Sirens range in length from a few centimetres to just under 1 m (3 ft). They have a streamlined body that moves easily through the water, small forelimbs and no hind limbs. They have eyes, but no eyelids. Sirens do not have any teeth at the front of their mouth. Instead they have a horny beak. The adults are unusual because they have large, external gills and gill slits.

KEY CHARACTERISTICS
SIRENOIDEA
- **No hind limbs and reduced forelimbs.**
- **Large, external gills.**
- **Horny beak instead of teeth at the front of the mouth.**

Habitat

Typically, sirens live in slow-moving water with lots of vegetation, such as ditches, swamps and lakes. They are active predators that hunt aquatic invertebrates. They pull their prey into their mouth using suction, which they create by expanding the size of their throat to create a vacuum. Sirens also eat aquatic plants.

Surviving droughts

Sirens are able to survive prolonged periods of drought by burrowing into the mud at the bottom of ponds. They wrap their body up in a protective cocoon formed from layers of skin cells. They leave their mouths uncovered so they can still breathe and remain cocooned in the mud for several months, waiting for it to rain.

Sirens, such as this Rio Grande lesser siren (*Siren intermedia texana*), have external gills and a long tail with a fin to aid swimming.

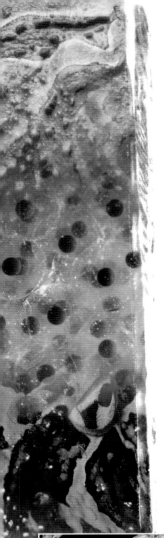

GIANT AND ASIATIC SALAMANDERS (CRYPTOBRANCHOIDEA)

THE SUPERFAMILY CRYPTOBRANCHOIDEA CONSISTS OF TWO families: giant salamanders (Cryptobranchidae) and Asiatic salamanders (Hynobiidae). Giant and Asiatic salamanders are large, tailed amphibians.

Giant salamanders

Giant salamanders have a massive head and body, and a relatively short tail. They do not have any eyelids. There are three species: the Chinese and Japanese giant salamanders, and the North American hellbender. All three species are aquatic, but unlike sirens, they do not use gills to breathe. Instead, a large fold of skin along the sides of their body increases the surface area for oxygen absorption and they use lungs to breathe.

Asiatic salamanders

Asiatic salamanders are considered to be the most ancient tailed amphibians. Some are terrestrial, while others live in fast-moving water. All species breed in streams. Their bodies are slender with a long tail and they have eyelids. Their lungs are either small or completely absent, so they breathe through their skin.

The Pacific giant salamander (*Dicamptodon ensatus*) has smooth, brownish-grey skin with black blotches, which camouflages it well on river beds, making it difficult to spot. When frightened, it makes a bark-like sound.

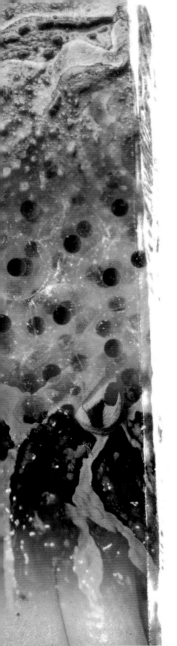

NEWTS AND SALAMANDERS (SALAMANDROIDEA)

NEWTS AND SALAMANDERS ARE A SUPERFAMILY OF TAILED amphibians. They are distinguished from the other superfamilies in the order Caudata by internal fertilization.

It can be easy to confuse an amphibian from this superfamily with a small lizard because they all have long tails. However, the amphibians can be identified by the number of digits on their forelimbs – newts and salamanders only have four digits whereas lizards have five. The term 'salamander' is generally used to describe a tailed amphibian that lives mostly on land, while a newt returns to water to breed.

Classification

The superfamily Salamandroidea contains about 54 species divided into seven families: Pacific mole salamanders; mole salamanders; newts and European salamanders; olms, mudpuppies and waterdogs; torrent salamanders; Congo eels; and lungless salamanders. The amphibians in each family are quite varied in their appearance and no one feature is present in them all apart from internal fertilization.

Mole salamanders are named after the fact that they spend much of their life in burrows. Olms, mudpuppies and waterdogs are aquatic amphibians, with feathery

Great crested newts (*Triturus cristatus*) return to water to breed. They have dark, grey-brown backs and sides covered with darker-coloured spots, which provide good camouflage in the dappled ponds where they breed.

gills and lungs. Olms live in caves. They are blind and lack any skin pigment. Lungless salamanders form the largest family. They do not have lungs and can only absorb oxygen through their skin and mouth. This limits their activity, so they are inactive for long periods of time. Lungless salamanders have to live in damp habitats so that their skin does not dry out. They are nocturnal (active at night).

Newts and European salamanders are a diverse family. Salamanders tend to have a smooth skin, while the skin of newts is rough. Most species have well-developed lungs. Most newts and European salamanders are small, rarely exceeding 20 cm (8 in) in length, and brightly coloured. They all produce toxins from their skin. Many of the most poisonous salamanders and newts, such as the American red spotted newt, have bright warning colours, which they use in defensive displays. Most newts spend several months in the water during the breeding season. European salamanders live in burrows, or under logs and stones in damp woodlands and sub-alpine meadows, emerging only on mild, damp nights.

KEY CHARACTERISTICS
SALAMANDROIDEA
- Presence of a tail.
- Internal fertilization.

The Northern red salamander (*Pseudotriton ruber*) is a lungless salamander found in the eastern states of the USA. It lives in woods and meadows close to clear, cool water.

Life cycles

Newts and salamanders follow one of three different life cycles: amphibious, terrestrial or aquatic.

Amphibious life cycle

Most newts and salamanders undergo an amphibious life cycle, in which eggs hatch as aquatic larvae with external gills and terrestrial adults breathe using lungs and/or their skin. Every spring, the adults return to water to breed. The adults spend several months in water, so their bodies change slightly to adapt to this habitat. Their skin becomes more permeable to oxygen, their tail becomes more flattened to aid swimming, their eyes change shape in order to focus in water, and they develop a line of sense organs in their skin that run from behind the head to the tail, which are sensitive to vibrations in the water. Sometimes, the males and females become more brightly coloured and carry out a courtship display.

Female newts and salamanders lay their eggs individually on leaves. The eggs hatch into larvae that are very similar in appearance to the tadpole larvae of frogs. The front legs appear first, quickly followed by the back legs. The external gills disappear and are replaced by lungs. Once the lungs form, the larvae go to the surface of the water to breathe. Then the rest of the body develops. When the eyes, digestive system and organs mature, the young newts or salamanders are ready to leave the water.

(Above) You can just see the tail of this newt embryo developing within an egg on the leaf of an aquatic plant. The newt larva develops within the egg and hatches after two to three weeks.

Newt larvae take about four months to metamorphose into adults. This is the larva of a great crested newt (*Triturus cristatus*).

14

Alpine newts (*Triturus alpestris*) develop bright breeding colours. The male (left) has blue markings and a prominent crest along its back. The female (right) has a mostly black body with an orange underside.

Terrestrial life cycle

A few species, such as the red-backed salamander, do not have an aquatic stage in their life cycle. Their eggs are laid under logs and develop directly into adults. The entire larval stage takes place within the egg and miniature adults emerge from the eggs.

NEWT LIFE CYCLE

Female great crested newts lay two or three eggs a day between March and mid-July, until 200–300 eggs have been laid. They lay the eggs on submerged aquatic plants, each one carefully wrapped up in a leaf. The larvae hatch after about three weeks and metamorphose into juveniles about four months later.

Aquatic life cycle

Some species, such as the axolotl, have an aquatic life cycle, in which the amphibian does not appear to metamorphose at all and keeps a larval appearance throughout its life. The axolotl spends its entire life underwater, apart from occasional trips to the surface to gulp a breath of air. Adult axolotls look just like large tadpoles, with three pairs of bushy gills at the back of their head. However, axolotls do go through metamorphosis, with the changes taking place inside the body and so hidden from view.

FROGS AND TOADS (ANURA)

THE ORDER ANURA IS THE LARGEST AND MOST DIVERSE of the amphibian orders. Frogs and toads are found all around the world except the Arctic and Antarctica, although most species live in the world's tropical regions.

The extra-long hind legs of this European toad (*Bufo bufo*) help to propel it through water. The toes are webbed to aid swimming.

KEY CHARACTERISTICS
ANURA

- Long back legs with elongated ankles.
- Short backbone.
- Most species lack ribs.
- Large, bulbous eyes.
- Wide mouth.

Anura features

There are about 4,750 species in this order, divided into 28 families. All frogs and toads have a body that is adapted to jumping. Their back legs are particularly long because their anklebones are enlarged to make an extra section in their leg. Their backbone is short and rigid to withstand the force of landing, and nearly all frogs and toads lack ribs. This is another adaptation to leaping since the force of landing would break any ribs.

Adult anurans, with a few exceptions, do not have a tail, although the tadpoles have a long tail that gets shorter as they go through metamorphosis. Their eyes are large and bulbous, and their mouth is wide. Virtually all frogs and toads have a long tongue to catch prey. Their eardrum is located behind their eyes, and they breathe using their lungs and through their moist skin.

Anurans have one of two basic body shapes, with their shape being an adaptation to their habitat. One group of anurans, such as European frogs, has a slender body with long back legs and a long head with a tapering snout. These frogs and toads tend to live in water and even when they go on land, they stay near water so they can jump back in when startled. Their streamlined bodies help them to swim and jump more easily. The second group includes those frogs and toads that live on land or burrow in the ground. They have squat bodies, shorter legs, and feet with stubby digits that are suitable for digging.

The order Anura is divided into two large suborders, known as Archaeobatrachia and Neobatrachia. Archaeobatrachians are featured on pages 20–23 and the Neobatrachians are on pages 24–41.

FROG OR TOAD?

There are no real differences between frogs and toads. Some species may be called frogs in some parts of the world and toads in others. Many people consider the drier, warty skin to be characteristic of the toad, but this is not always the case.

Tree frogs are adapted to living in trees by having large digits on their feet to help them to grip. This species (*Hyla lindae*) is found in the rainforests of western Ecuador.

This African bullfrog male (*Pyxicephalus adspersus*) is digging a channel to another pool of water in order to rescue its tadpoles that are stranded in a shrinking pool of water.

Habitats

Most frogs and toads that live in temperate regions of the world are not active during the winter months. Since they are ectothermic, they rely on heat from their environment to keep their bodies warm so in the cold winter months they go into a deep sleep, called torpor. In torpor, they do not use up energy to stay warm, so they are able to survive without having to eat. Those species that live in very cold environments, such as Siberia, have a natural antifreeze in their bodies to prevent ice forming in their cells.

At the other extreme, frogs and toads that live in deserts face a different set of problems. During the dry season, when their pools dry up, these frogs survive by aestivating. They dig themselves into the mud until the rains start again. Their bodies dehydrate, or lose water, to the mud. When the rains return, they rehydrate, or reabsorb water. Some desert-living species have water-storage organs inside their bodies, which keep them alive during aestivation. When it rains, temporary pools form and the frogs immediately emerge from the mud, mate and lay their eggs. Their tadpoles must complete their metamorphosis in the short time that the water remains in the pools. Once the water dries up, any tadpoles that have not matured into adult frogs die.

Food and hunting

Frogs and toads are predators. They hunt a range of small prey animals, such as worms, slugs, snails, beetles, flies and spiders. They catch smaller prey by flicking out their long, sticky tongue and grip larger prey with their jaws and their backward-facing teeth.

Camouflage and warning colours

Frogs and toads are the prey of many animals, and they have a variety of ways to avoid predators. Some rely on camouflage, using a skin colour that blends in with their surroundings. Poisonous species rely on warning colours, using their bright colours to warn predators that they are poisonous.

This false-eyed frog from South America is showing the two large eye-spots on its back in an attempt to defend itself.

FALSE EYES
The false-eyed frog has a pair of bright spots on its back that look like enormous eyes. When resting, the frog's thighs cover these eye-spots, but when a predator approaches, the frog lowers its head and lifts its back, creating the illusion of a much larger, scarier head than its own.

ARCHAEOBATRACHIANS (ARCHAEOBATRACHIA)

The tiny tail of this tailed frog (*Ascaphus truei*) can just be seen. Only the males have this tail and they use it to fertilize the eggs inside the female. Tailed frogs lack an eardrum that is present in other frogs.

THE SUBORDER ARCHAEOBATRACHIA IS MADE UP OF NINE families of relatively ancient frogs and toads. There are about 150 species, some of which are found in just one or two places in the world. The frogs and toads in each family differ from each other internally and by their method of reproduction.

Tailed frogs

Tailed frogs are the oldest family of frogs. They are unusual because the adults have a short tail. They also have free ribs in their chest (ribs that are not attached to the breast bone). There are only two species of tailed frogs, living in fast-flowing mountain streams of North America. These nocturnal frogs show a number of adaptations to fast-flowing water. The males have extra-large forearms to grip the female when mating, so that she is not swept away by the water! The eggs are laid in strings under rocks, where they are out of the current. Living in a cold environment slows down their rate of growth so these frogs take several years to metamorphose and they are not ready to breed before they are seven years old.

Firebellied toads

The most distinguishing feature of firebellied toads is their brightly coloured undersides, which are orange or red with black spots. These are warning colours to let predators know they are distasteful. When threatened, firebellied toads lift up their body to reveal their coloured underside.

Midwife toads

Midwife toads are small, squat toads with a rough skin, found in Europe. They are mostly terrestrial, even mating on land. The female lays a long string of eggs, which the male catches and wraps around his hind legs. The male carries the eggs around for several weeks until they are ready to hatch, when he takes them to a pool. By carrying the eggs with him, the male protects them from predators and disease so that more tadpoles will hatch out.

FAMILIES
ARCHAEOBATRACHIA

The nine families in the suborder Archaeobatrachia are:

- **Tailed frogs (Ascaphidae)**
- **New Zealand frogs (Leiopelmatidae)**
- **Fire-bellied toads (Bombinatoridae)**
- **Midwife toads (Discoglossidae)**
- **Asian toadfrogs (Megophryidae)**
- **Spadefoot toads (Pelobatidae)**
- **Parsley frogs (Pelodytidae)**
- **Clawed frogs and Surinam toads (Pipidae)**
- **Mexican burrowing frogs (Rhinophrynidae)**

The male midwife toad (*Alytes obstetricans*) carries the yellow strands of eggs on his back for about 30 days. During this time he cannot mate with other females. The females continue to produce eggs, which are carried around by other males.

Asian toadfrogs

Asian toadfrogs are found living near streams in Southeast Asia. Their tadpoles are adapted for life in streams. They have large, sucker-like mouths to hang on to the surfaces of rocks, to stop them being carried away by the current. Malaysian horned toads have horn-like growths above their eyes and on their nose. Their body is mottled brown and green, which provides perfect camouflage on the forest floor.

Spadefoot toads

Spadefoot toads live in dry areas and deserts of Europe and Western Asia. They are nocturnal, only coming out at night when it is cooler to hunt insects and spiders. During the day they shelter in burrows, where it is cooler. During the hottest times of the

SPADEFOOT TOADS

Spadefoot toads have hard growths on their hind feet. These claw-like 'spades' help them to dig cool, underground burrows in the dry habitats where they live. Unlike most animals, spadefoot toads dig backwards. While digging with their hind feet, they move in a backward spiral and gradually disappear into the earth.

Spadefoot toads, such as this plains spadefoot (*Scaphiopus bombifrons*), are named after the small, black 'spade' on the first toe of each hind foot. This hardened pad allows them to dig into the loose soil without damaging their toes.

year, spadefoot toads retreat into deep burrows, where they stay for several months. Although they lose a lot of water from their bodies, they are able to survive. Spadefoot toads breed after the rains have arrived and some of their tadpoles can metamorphose into young toads in just three weeks.

Clawed frogs and Surinam toads

These toads are fully aquatic, so their bodies are adapted to living in water. Their bodies are flattened and their legs stick out sideways, an arrangement that is good for swimming but hopeless for walking on land. Their feet are webbed to help swimming and even their eyes point upwards so that they can see animals moving in the water above them. Clawed frogs and Surinam toads are very unusual because they don't have tongues. They feed on the larvae of aquatic insects and small fish, which they catch and shovel into their wide mouth using their feet.

Surinam toads have an unusual life cycle, without a free-swimming larval stage. The life cycle starts when the male grips the female to mate. The female lays her eggs, which the male fertilizes and then sweeps up with his feet and places on the female's back. The eggs stick to her back and become embedded in her skin. When the eggs hatch into tadpoles, they stay in a pocket in the female's skin. Several months later, tiny toadlets emerge and leave their mother.

The African clawed frog (*Xenopus laevis*) is an aquatic species that spends its life in water. Its front feet are unwebbed, but its back feet are webbed with sharp black claws on the inner toes.

23

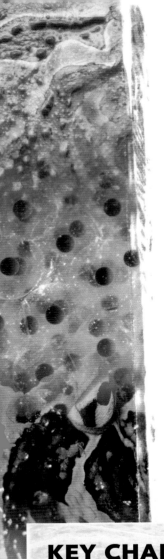

LEPTODACTYLIDS (LEPTODACTYLIDAE)

THIS IS A LARGE FAMILY OF FROGS THAT ARE FOUND throughout Central and South America, the southern parts of North America, and on islands in the Caribbean.

The family Leptodactylidae is part of the suborder Neobatrachia (see page 44). There are 864 species, including the false-eyed and the white-lipped frogs. Some are relatively large frogs, about 25 cm (10 in) long, but there are a few tiny species as well.

Shared features

All the frogs in this family have a particularly wide mouth and teeth on their upper jaw. Some species, such as the Brazilian horned frog, have a horned appearance due to the presence of horn-like flaps above their eyes.

The Amazon horned frog (*Ceratophrys cornuta*) has small horns above its eyes. It digs itself under leaf litter so that just its head sticks out and waits for prey to pass by. Then it jumps out and swallows the prey in one swift snap of its mouth.

KEY CHARACTERISTICS
LEPTODACTYLIDAE

■ **Teeth on upper jaw.**
■ **Wide mouth.**

Subfamilies

Leptodactylidae is split into four subfamilies: Ceratophryinae, Hylodinae, Leptodactylinae and Telmatobiinae. Ceratophryinae is a small group of large-headed, aggressive, carnivorous frogs. The Leptodactylinae are mostly terrestrial but some live in trees where they build foam nests for their eggs. The adults secrete mucus from their skin and reproductive tracts, which they beat into a foam with their legs. The eggs are laid in the foam nest, which protects them from drying up. In several species, one of the parents stays close to the nest to protect it.

The Lake Titicaca frog (*Telmatobius culeus*) is the largest aquatic frog in the world. About 30 years ago it was possible to find some of these frogs that were 30 cm (12 in) in length and weighed 1 kg (2.2 lb). Unfortunately, the large frogs have been collected for food and today Lake Titicaca frogs are much smaller.

Surviving in the Andes

Some frogs in the subfamily Telmatobiinae live in mountain lakes high up in the Andes mountains of Peru and Bolivia, at altitudes of 4,000 m (13,124 ft). These frogs have to cope with cold air and water, low oxygen levels and high levels of ultraviolet radiation (the harmful rays in sunlight that can cause skin cancers in people). One extraordinary frog is the Lake Titicaca frog, which has adaptations to help it survive in its low-oxygen environment. Its extra-baggy skin absorbs more oxygen, which allows the frog to stay submerged for long periods of time. This means it does not have to come to the surface, where it is exposed to ultraviolet radiation. Lake Titicaca frogs move their hind legs around to create small disturbances in the water, which brings fresh oxygenated water closer to their bodies. Their blood is unique, too, because it has the smallest red blood cells of any amphibian, and the highest amount of haemoglobin. Haemoglobin is found in red blood cells and its job is to pick up oxygen, so the more haemoglobin an animal has, the more oxygen it can carry in its blood.

TRUE TOADS AND HARLEQUIN FROGS (BUFONIDAE)

TRUE TOADS AND HARLEQUIN FROGS ARE FOUND ACROSS North and South America, Africa, Europe and Asia. Most species are terrestrial, although some live much of their lives in streams, and a few are found in trees.

Shared features

There are about 376 species in the family Bufonidae, ranging in size from 1–25 cm (0.3–10 in) in length. All species have a pair of poison glands, which ooze a poisonous, milky fluid to deter predators. The poison is stronger in some species than others, but even in its mildest form it causes a burning sensation if it gets in the eyes or mouth of a predator. The secretion is particularly toxic in the brightly coloured harlequin frogs, whose warning colours show that they are poisonous.

True toads

The term 'true toads' refers to species that belong to the family Bufonidae. Most move by hopping and crawling rather than leaping. They have thick, warty skins, a stout, short body and relatively short, thick legs.

Harlequin frogs

Harlequin frogs differ from most toads because they have a slender body and long legs. They lay their eggs in fast-flowing streams. Their tadpoles are adapted to this moving environment by having suckers on their abdomens, which grip the surface of rocks and stop them being carried away.

The male harlequin frog (*Atelopus varius*) does not call. It attracts females using visual displays such as leg and head twitching, stamping the ground, or hopping on the spot.

Breeding

True toads breed in ponds. Many species take part in mass migrations to their breeding ponds every year. In early spring, thousands of European toads are seen crossing roads to reach their breeding ponds. They follow the same route every year. Once they reach the ponds, the toads form pairs. The male grips the female as she lays eggs and the eggs are fertilized externally. In most toads, the eggs are laid in long chains in water, although a few species lay their eggs on leaves above the water.

Problem toads

Most toads are considered to be useful animals because they eat large numbers of insects and slugs, which are pests in gardens and among crops. In 1935, cane toads were introduced to Queensland, Australia to control insect pests in the sugar-cane fields. However, the plan backfired. The introduced toads ate both pests and beneficial insects, and soon the toad numbers increased to pest levels. Cane toads are now hunted in an attempt to stop them invading new habitats, where they threaten the survival of native species.

The cane toad (*Bufo marinus*) has a poisonous skin secretion that can sicken or kill animals that bite or try to eat it, including dogs, cats, small mammals and snakes.

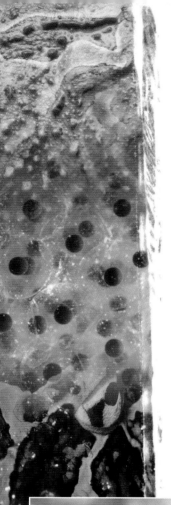

POISON FROGS (DENDROBATIDAE)

THESE SMALL, BRIGHTLY COLOURED FROGS ARE ALSO called poison-arrow or poison-dart frogs because some Amerindian tribes in South America rub their blowgun darts over the backs of the species *Phyllobates terribilis* to smear them with poison. However, not all frogs in this family are poisonous.

Shared features

There are about 170 different species of poison frogs, including the strawberry frog and the blue poison-dart frog. They are all small, ranging in size from 2–4 cm (1–1.5 in). They have slender limbs, and toes with adhesive pads for gripping.

Most of these frogs are brightly coloured as a visible warning that they are incredibly poisonous. The poison oozes out of pores in their skin. There are three species that are extremely dangerous. The deadliest is *Phyllobates terribilis*. Its poison is called batrachotoxin and the poison from one frog is enough to kill 20,000 mice or eight humans. Interestingly, poison frogs are not so poisonous when they are kept in captivity, so scientists believe that they gain their poison from the insects they eat.

The yellow and blue poison frog (*Dendrobates tinctorius*) is one of the larger of the poison frogs, reaching up to 5 cm (2 in) long.

KEY CHARACTERISTICS
DENDROBATIDAE
■ Toxic skin secretions.

Habitat

Poison frogs are found in the tropical rainforests of Central and South America, where they come out by day and hop along the forest floor. In these forests, the air temperature and humidity stay much the same all year round. This is important to poison frogs because they require a humidity of at least 80 per cent. If the humidity drops, these tiny frogs can dry up and die within a few hours. The temperature has to be about 22 °C (72 °F), although some species can live in cool, humid forests on mountain slopes.

Breeding

Female poison frogs lay a small clutch of three to five eggs on leaves on the ground. When the eggs hatch, usually the male carries the tadpoles on his back, one by one, to a stream or pool of water. Sometimes the male chooses a tiny pool of water trapped in the leaves of plants such as bromeliads. The females of some poison frog species lay unfertilized eggs as food for their tadpoles. The males can be territorial, guarding an area of the forest floor. If another male intrudes, there may be a fight, with the males wrestling each other using their back legs. Strawberry poison frogs are very territorial and a male will defend his territory to the death.

A chemical from the phantasmal frog (*Epipedobates tricolor*) is about 200 times more effective than morphine in laboratory tests. Researchers are hoping to mimic its effects to develop medicines to block pain.

TREE FROGS (HYLIDAE)

HYLIDAE IS A LARGE FAMILY OF FROGS THAT ARE ADAPTED to life in trees. They are found in North and South America, Europe, the northern tip of Africa, Southeast Asia and Australia.

There are over 700 species of tree frogs, including marsupial frogs, chorus frogs and leaf frogs. Most tree frogs live in trees and can jump from branch to branch. However, some species are aquatic, while others spend their lives on the ground. Most species are small frogs, under 6 cm (2 in) in length, but there are a couple of species that can grow up to 14 cm (5.5 in) long.

Shared features

Tree frogs have a slender, slightly flattened body with long, thin legs. They have horizontal pupils and webbed feet. The ends of their toes are enlarged to form adhesive pads, which they use for gripping and climbing. Tree frogs also have extra segments of cartilage between the last two

The red-eyed tree frog (*Agalychnis callidryas*) has very obvious red eyes. During the day, the frog sleeps with its eyes closed so that its green body blends in better with its surroundings. If disturbed, it opens its huge red eyes to scare off any predators.

bones of each toe, which allow their toes to swivel and keep flat against all surfaces. Some tree frogs have elaborate skull bones that form a kind of helmet, called a casque. Casque-headed frogs use their helmet to seal the entrances to their burrows, to reduce the amount of water lost by evaporation.

KEY CHARACTERISTICS
HYLIDAE
- Slender body and long, thin legs.
- Enlarged toes that form adhesive discs.
- Horizontal pupils.

Breeding

Since tree frogs are arboreal (live in trees), most species lay their eggs on leaves in trees. Leaf frogs lay clusters of eggs on leaves above pools of water. The female frog keeps the eggs moist by urinating on them until they hatch. Then the tadpoles drop into pools below. Other tree frogs lay their eggs in a protective nest of foam. The adult frogs whip up mucus into a foam with their back legs, into which the female lays her eggs. The foam hardens and protects the eggs. When the tadpoles hatch, they wiggle free of the nest and drop into water below.

Marsupial frogs

Marsupial frogs carry their young in a pouch, just like marsupial mammals such as kangaroos. The female Australian marsupial frog (*Assa darlingtoni*) deposits a few large eggs into moist soil. When they hatch, the male stands over them and the tiny tadpoles wiggle into slit-like openings on his hips. These act as pouches in which the tadpoles are carried around. Only about half the tadpoles make it to the safety of the pouches. The male carries the tadpoles for about 48–69 days, until their metamorphosis is complete and young frogs emerge from the male's skin. In other species of marsupial frog, the female carries the tadpoles.

The embryos inside these common tree frog eggs are developing underwater. The common tree frog (*Hyla arborea*) lives among trees and bushes for much of the year, but lays its eggs in shallow water. The female lays clusters of up to 50 eggs, with each egg measuring about 2 mm (0.08 in) in diameter.

GLASS FROGS (CENTROLENIDAE)

GLASS FROGS ARE FOUND IN TROPICAL PARTS OF CENTRAL and South America. The greatest number of species are found in the rainforests of Costa Rica and Panama, and on the forested slopes of the Andes.

The family Centrolenidae contains 104 species, including the reticulated and emerald glass frogs. However, as more rainforests are explored, even more species of glass frogs are being discovered.

Shared features

Glass frogs were named after the fact that their skin is partly transparent, so their internal organs are visible. On their upper surface they tend to be green with yellow, white, blue or red markings. Most species are smaller than 3 cm (1 in) in length, although a few species reach just under 8 cm (3 in). They have a small, but wide body and a blunt head. Their small eyes lie almost on the top of the head.

It is just possible to make out the bones and digestive system of this glass frog (*Hyalinobatrachium sp.*) as it sits on a rainforest leaf.

This male glass frog (*Centrolenella fleischmanni*) is guarding its eggs. Parental care ensures that more of the tadpoles will hatch.

KEY CHARACTERISTICS
CENTROLENIDAE
- ■ **Partly transparent skin.**
- ■ **Blunt head.**
- ■ **Extra leg section with one bone rather than two.**

Glass frogs have horizontal pupils and, like many other tree-living frogs, they have enlarged toes for gripping. Glass frogs have an extra section in their legs, but unlike other Anuran families, it is made up of just one bone rather than two.

Egg laying

Glass frogs live high in trees near mountain streams. Like many other types of tree frog, they lay their eggs on leaves that overhang streams. Many species show parental care, with the male frogs guarding small clutches of eggs after they have been laid. When the eggs hatch, the tadpoles fall into the water below, where they live in the mud and leaf litter at the bottom of streams. This habitat is low in oxygen. The tadpoles' blood flows very close to the surface of their skin so it can pick up as much oxygen as possible. Since their skin is partly transparent, the colour of the blood shows through the skin, giving the tadpoles of these frogs a bright red appearance.

Male glass frogs are territorial. They defend a small area of the forest from other frogs of the same species. In particular, they guard the places from which they make their calls to attract females. The call of a glass frog is a high peep or whistle. In some species, the call of a single frog may imitate a chorus to attract more females.

TRUE FROGS (RANIDAE)

TRUE FROGS ARE FOUND IN ALMOST EVERY HABITAT apart from the very cold. They are found all around the world, including islands in the Caribbean.

Shared features

The family Ranidae contains 643 species, including the common frog, wood frog, goliath frog and edible frog. They range in size from 2–30 cm (1–12 in) long. True frogs are characterized by long, muscular hind limbs, which usually end in webbed feet. Their long legs and webbed feet help these frogs to swim. Their body has a slender, streamlined shape. The head is pointed and their eyes are large and bulbous, with horizontal pupils. They have teeth on their upper jaws. Their skin is usually smooth, although a few have a slightly warty skin. The colour of their skin is usually a combination of browns and greens, which blends well with the ground and provides good camouflage.

Habitat

Most true frogs are terrestrial, living out of water for much of the year. They move around by hopping and jumping. Some species can tolerate brackish water, that is, water that is partly fresh and partly salt. The crab-eating frog can survive in salty mangrove swamps.

The African bullfrog (*Pyxicephalus adspersus*) has three large teeth sticking out from its lower jaw, which it uses to fight off predators and hold on to its prey. This bullfrog is eating a mouse.

Life cycle

Most true frogs have an amphibious life cycle, spending time on land but returning to water to lay their eggs. However, there are a few species that lay their eggs on land, and the eggs hatch directly into tiny adults.

Most species lay clumps of eggs, called frog spawn, in water. The eggs hatch into free-swimming tadpoles. Some species of frogs lay their eggs in flowing water. Their tadpoles have discs on their abdomen to grip stones on the riverbed so they are not washed away.

Some species of frogs, such as the European common frog, gather together in large numbers during the breeding season. The females lay their eggs in clumps beside those of other females. It is thought that the clumps help the eggs survive cold weather. The thick layer of jelly in the egg acts as insulation, while the black embryo in the middle absorbs heat from the sun. Together these features mean that the temperature in a clump of eggs can be several degrees warmer than the surrounding water, which is just enough to stop them freezing during a cold spring night.

KEY CHARACTERISTICS
RANIDAE

- Long, muscular hind limbs with webbed feet.
- Streamlined shape.
- Teeth on upper jaw.

It was thought that the male holding the female common frog (*Rana temporaria*) as she lay her eggs fertilized all the eggs in the clutch. However, new research has found that other males release their sperm over the eggs after the first male frog has gone, so the eggs are often fertilized by more than one male.

REED AND SEDGE FROGS (HYPEROLIIDAE)

REED AND SEDGE FROGS ARE FOUND IN AFRICA, Madagascar and the Seychelles. They are arboreal frogs that have bright, distinctive markings. The family Hyperoliidae contains 234 species, including bush frogs, marbled reed frogs and sedge frogs.

Shared features

Reed and sedge frogs are relatively small frogs, measuring about 2–9 cm (1–3 in) long. They have slender, streamlined bodies without any ribs, and moderately long legs. Their toes have enlarged discs for gripping, their eyes have horizontal pupils and they have teeth on their upper jaws. Many species have smooth, brightly patterned, almost metallic-looking skin.

Reed and sedge frogs are nocturnal, emerging at night to feed on a variety of prey animals such as insects, spiders and slugs. Some species, such as *Tornierella sp.*, specialize in eating just snails, while *Afrixalus fornasinii* preys on the eggs of other species of frogs.

This painted reed frog (*Hyperolius marmoratus*) is just 12 mm (0.47 in) long. Its call is a shrill, high-pitched whistle so when a group of these frogs start to call the sound can be deafening.

Egg-laying

Reed and sedge frogs resemble tree frogs in many ways. For example, most live in trees and lay their eggs on branches that overhang water. Some sedge frogs lay their eggs in holes in trees. A few lay their eggs on the ground so that after they hatch, the tadpoles have to wiggle over the ground to reach water.

Colour change

Some reed and sedge frogs are able to change the colour of their skin. In some species, the skin colour varies with the temperature of the surroundings. Some species of reed frogs, including the spiny reed frog, which is found in dry habitats in Africa, range in colour from almost-white in the hot season through to copper at cooler times of the year. The paler skin reflects the sun's heat, which helps to keep the frog cool and reduce water loss. The arum lily frog lives in wetlands in South Africa. These frogs are sometimes found in white arum lily flowers, where they change their skin colour to white to match their surroundings. This makes them virtually invisible to predators as well as to their insect prey. When the flowers die, the frogs turn brown to match.

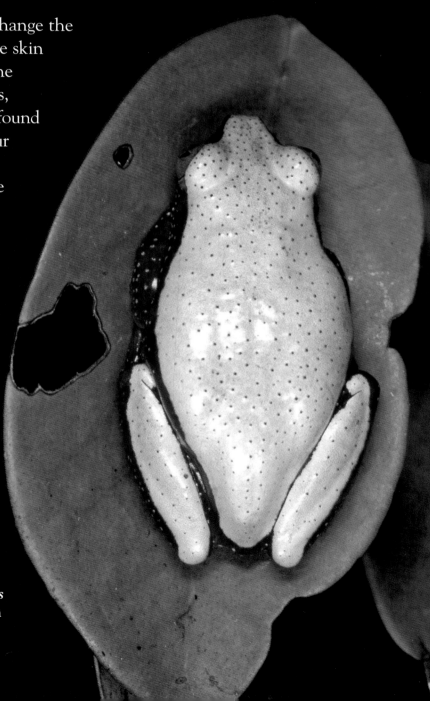

This spiny reed frog (*Afrixalus fornasinii*) has turned white in the sunlight. Its normal skin colour is brown.

OLD WORLD TREE FROGS (RHACOPHORIDAE)

OLD WORLD TREE FROGS ARE FOUND IN TROPICAL PARTS of Africa, Madagascar, and across Asia from India to Japan, including the islands of Southeast Asia.

This family contains about 276 species, including grey tree frogs, Madagascan mantellas and Wallace's flying frogs. They range in size from only 1.5–12 cm (0.6–5 in) long. Most of these frogs are arboreal, although there are a few terrestrial species.

Madagascan mantellas such as this golden mantella (*Mantella aurantiac*) look very similar to the poison frogs of South America. However it has been proved that these two families of frogs evolved completely separately.

Shared features

Most old world tree frogs have webbed feet, and the webs are often brightly coloured. In some species, the webs between the feet are enlarged to help the frog glide from tree to tree. Like all tree frogs, members of this family have enlarged discs on their toes for gripping branches. They have teeth on their upper jaws and their pupils are horizontal.

Mantella frogs

The Mantella frogs of Madagascar are similar to the poison frogs of South America, although they are not closely related. Like poison frogs, mantella frogs are poisonous and have bright warning colours. Their poison comes from the plants they eat and oozes from their skin. However,

Mantella frogs are not as poisonous as poison frogs. If a person were to handle a Mantella frog and then touch their mouth, the worst effect would be for their lips to go numb.

Mantella frogs tend to live near bamboo plants. The males are violently territorial and will defend an area of up to 2 m² (6.6 ft²) around a 'well' of water, such as a rain-filled stalk of broken bamboo. When a female answers the call of a chirping male, the male leads her to his well. If she likes the well the female lays one egg, which the male fertilizes. Then she attaches the egg to the side of the well, above the water level. The egg hatches in about 10 days and the tadpole drops into the water. The female visits the tadpole regularly to lay unfertilized eggs for the tadpole to eat.

Flying frogs

Wallace's flying frogs have feet with extra-large webbing, which act as a parachute. These nocturnal, gliding frogs can even make sharp turns in mid-air. Gliding is an efficient way to move about. The frogs can descend quickly from the highest branches to breeding sites near the forest floor. They can also glide from tree to tree without having to come down to the forest floor, where they are at risk from predators.

KEY CHARACTERISTICS
RHACOPHORIDAE

- Broad, flat skull.
- Webbed feet.
- Enlarged discs on toes for gripping.
- Teeth on their upper jaw.
- Horizontal pupils.

The Wallace's flying frog (*Rhacophorus nigropalmatus*) can glide for distances of up to 45 m (148 ft). Like most tree frogs, it has pads on its toes to help it to grip when it lands.

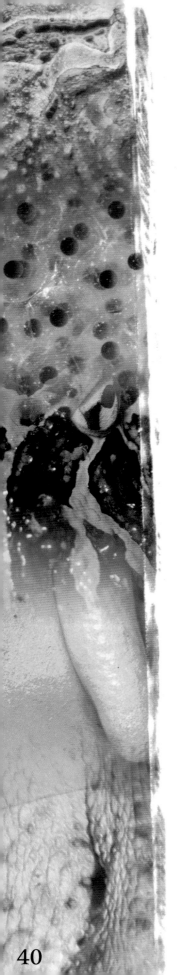

NARROW-MOUTHED FROGS (MICROHYLIDAE)

NARROW-MOUTHED FROGS ARE FOUND IN TROPICAL regions of the world, such as Central and South America, central and southern Africa, parts of India and across Southeast Asia.

There are more than 400 species in the narrow-mouthed frog family, including the tomato frog, rain frog and sheep frog. They range in size from just 1–10 cm (0.4–4 in). Most species are nocturnal. Their habitat varies from wet, tropical rainforest to arid desert and savannah. Many of these frogs are arboreal, but some species are terrestrial. The terrestrial species spend the day sheltering in burrows and emerge at night to feed.

Shared features
Narrow-mouthed frogs have a small, pointed head with a narrow mouth, a rounded body and short legs. They do not have webbed feet, have no teeth, and most have eyes with horizontal pupils.

Rain frogs such as this Namaqua rain frog (*Breviceps namaquensis*) burrow into the ground during dry weather. They are named after the way they come to the surface after rain, when the males call to the females.

Breeding

Narrow-mouthed frogs lay their eggs either in water, in burrows, or in the tiny pools of water trapped inside the leaves of bromeliads. During mating, most males grip the female around her middle. However, an African species called breviceps is so round and short-legged that it is impossible for the male to grip the female. Instead, he secretes a sticky substance that glues him to the female. Breviceps frogs build a foam nest in which the female lays her eggs.

Tomato frogs (*Dyscophus sp.*) are terrestrial and live in forest habitats. Many of the forests on Madagascar have been cleared, but this frog has adapted well to living on farmland and even in gardens.

Tomato frogs

Most species of narrow-mouthed frogs have a brown or grey body but a few, such as tomato frogs, are brightly coloured. Tomato frogs are found on Madagascar. Their bright colour acts as a warning. These frogs are not poisonous, but they can produce a sticky white mucus that irritates the skin, which is thought to deter predators. Apart from using their mucus, tomato frogs can also deter predators by inflating their bodies like a balloon.

KEY CHARACTERISTICS
MICROHYLIDAE
- ■ Small pointed head.
- ■ Rounded body.
- ■ Relatively short legs.

The frog and the spider

Some species of narrow-mouthed frogs living in South America have a strange relationship with theraphosid spiders, a type of tarantula. One such species is *Chiasmocleis ventrimaculata*. These frogs live in the burrows of theraphosid spiders, which is quite risky because the spiders normally prey on small frogs, but for some reason they tolerate this particular species. The frogs share the spiders' burrows during the day and emerge at night to feed. In some cases, the frogs have been seen hiding under the spiders when threatened by a predator. The frogs benefit from the protection offered by the spiders, but nobody is sure how the spiders benefit.

UNDER THREAT

NEW SPECIES OF AMPHIBIANS ARE BEING DISCOVERED ALL the time, especially small species that live in rainforests. However, hundreds of other species are either becoming extinct or are under the threat of extinction.

Environmental damage

One of the main reasons for the global decline in amphibians is the loss of their habitats. Rainforests are being cleared at an ever-increasing rate, and wetland habitats and ponds are disappearing, too.

Another major threat is global warming. One of the effects of global warming is climate change and extreme weather events such as droughts, storms and flooding. Amphibians are very sensitive to changes in their surroundings and cannot tolerate a change in the climate, however small.

Acid rain can affect amphibians, too. Acid rain is rain that contains pollutants such as sulphur dioxide and nitrogen oxides, which make the rain more acidic than normal. When acid rain falls on ponds, lakes and rivers, it makes the water more acidic, which harms the eggs of amphibians.

Pesticides harm amphibians in different ways. Weedkillers or insecticides are sometimes accidentally sprayed on amphibians. In some places, frogs have been found with deformed legs and strange pigmentation, which has been linked to the use of pesticides. When insects, slugs

Some ponds and streams are polluted by fertilizers and sewage that add nutrients to the water. This can lead to massive growths of algae, which disrupts the food chains of frogs and toads, forcing them to move away.

and snails are killed by pesticides, amphibians lose their food source. They may also eat prey that has been sprayed by pesticides and be poisoned themselves.

Disease

Disease is killing thousands of frogs around the world. In Britain, common frogs are dying from a disease called red leg. This is a fungal disease that spreads from pond to pond, killing all the frogs. Frogs are dying from similar fungal diseases in North and South America, and Australia, too.

Conservation

One of the best ways to conserve amphibians is to protect existing habitats and create new ones. New amphibian habitats can be created by clearing waste from ponds and ditches, and building new ponds in gardens and on farmland. A simple pile of logs can provide amphibians with shelter for the winter.

Many toads are killed on roads every year during their annual migration to their breeding ponds. In some places, where toads are known to cross every year, special tunnels have been built under busy roads for the toads to cross safely. In other places, local people protect the toads by carrying them across the roads during the breeding season. However, for the very rare species, the only way to ensure their survival is to breed them in captivity.

A toad tunnel was built under this road to allow toads to reach their breeding ponds safely. Many countries build tunnels under new roads to allow toads, frogs, and mammals such as badgers to cross safely underneath.

BRED IN CAPTIVITY

One of the rarest amphibians, the Mallorcan midwife toad, has been rescued from the brink of extinction by being bred in captivity. This toad was once considered to be extinct, but in 1980, a few toads were discovered living in the mountains of Mallorca, Spain. Twenty toads were moved to Jersey Zoo where they were bred and in 1989, 76 toads were released back into the wild in Mallorca. Today Mallorcan midwife toads have been reclassified as 'vulnerable' rather than 'critically endangered'.

AMPHIBIAN CLASSIFICATION

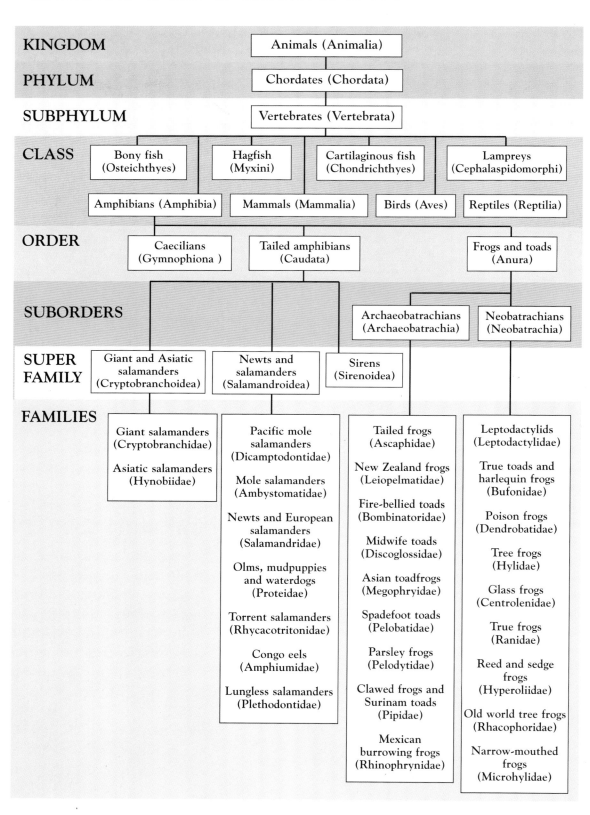

KINGDOM	Animals (Animalia)
PHYLUM	Chordates (Chordata)
SUBPHYLUM	Vertebrates (Vertebrata)

CLASS
- Bony fish (Osteichthyes)
- Hagfish (Myxini)
- Cartilaginous fish (Chondrichthyes)
- Lampreys (Cephalaspidomorphi)
- Amphibians (Amphibia)
- Mammals (Mammalia)
- Birds (Aves)
- Reptiles (Reptilia)

ORDER
- Caecilians (Gymnophiona)
- Tailed amphibians (Caudata)
- Frogs and toads (Anura)

SUBORDERS
- Archaeobatrachians (Archaeobatrachia)
- Neobatrachians (Neobatrachia)

SUPER FAMILY
- Giant and Asiatic salamanders (Cryptobranchoidea)
- Newts and salamanders (Salamandroidea)
- Sirens (Sirenoidea)

FAMILIES

- Giant salamanders (Cryptobranchidae)
- Asiatic salamanders (Hynobiidae)

- Pacific mole salamanders (Dicamptodontidae)
- Mole salamanders (Ambystomatidae)
- Newts and European salamanders (Salamandridae)
- Olms, mudpuppies and waterdogs (Proteidae)
- Torrent salamanders (Rhycacotritonidae)
- Congo eels (Amphiumidae)
- Lungless salamanders (Plethodontidae)

- Tailed frogs (Ascaphidae)
- New Zealand frogs (Leiopelmatidae)
- Fire-bellied toads (Bombinatoridae)
- Midwife toads (Discoglossidae)
- Asian toadfrogs (Megophryidae)
- Spadefoot toads (Pelobatidae)
- Parsley frogs (Pelodytidae)
- Clawed frogs and Surinam toads (Pipidae)
- Mexican burrowing frogs (Rhinophrynidae)

- Leptodactylids (Leptodactylidae)
- True toads and harlequin frogs (Bufonidae)
- Poison frogs (Dendrobatidae)
- Tree frogs (Hylidae)
- Glass frogs (Centrolenidae)
- True frogs (Ranidae)
- Reed and sedge frogs (Hyperoliidae)
- Old world tree frogs (Rhacophoridae)
- Narrow-mouthed frogs (Microhylidae)

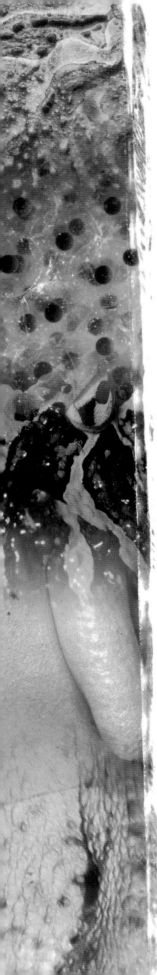

GLOSSARY

abdomen The part of the body of a vertebrate that lies between the thorax (chest) and the pelvic girdle (hips).

acid rain Rain containing acid formed in the atmosphere from industrial waste gases.

adaptation A change in order to suit the environment.

aestivating Being dormant during a period of hot weather.

Amerindians The people living in North and South America before the Europeans arrived.

antifreeze A substance that stops water from freezing.

aquatic Living in water.

arboreal Living in trees.

beneficial Having a good effect.

breed To reproduce.

breeding season The time of year when animals mate and lay their eggs.

bromeliads Plants that live on trees in rainforests.

bulbous Rounded, swollen and bulb-like in shape.

camouflage Colours and patterns that blend with the surroundings.

carnivorous Meat-eating animals.

cartilage A tough, elastic substance forming part of the skeleton in vertebrates.

characteristic A feature of an animal, for example having webbed feet or a wide mouth.

dehydrate To lose water.

digits Fingers or toes.

ectothermic Having a body temperature that rises and falls with the outside temperature, often referred to as cold-blooded.

embryo An early stage of a vertebrate's life before it is born.

extinct No longer living.

eye-spots Rounded, eye-like markings.

fertilization The fusing of an egg (from the female) and sperm (from the male) to form a zygote, a new individual.

fungal Relating to or caused by a fungus. A fungus is a group of organisms that feed on organic matter.

gill The part of the body that an aquatic animal uses to take up oxygen from water.

gill slits Narrow, external openings of the body through which water passes from the gills to the outside.

habitats The places where animals or plants live.

haemoglobin A large protein containing iron that picks up oxygen.

humidity Moisture in the air.

insecticides Chemicals used to kill insect pests.

invertebrates Animals that do not have a backbone, for example insects and snails.

Jacobson's organ A sensory organ in the roof of an amphibian's mouth.

juveniles Young, immature adults.

larva A young animal that looks different from the adult and changes shape as it grows.

Glossary

metamorphosis The process of changing appearance, for example the development of a larval animal into an adult.

migration A regular journey between two different places at certain times of year, in order to feed or breed, for example.

mucus A sticky substance consisting of water and protein.

nocturnal Active at night.

oxygenated Enriched or supplied with oxygen.

permeable Able to allow liquids and gases to pass through.

pesticides Chemicals used to kill pests such as insects, fungi or weeds.

pigment A substance that produces a characteristic colour in a plant or animal tissue.

predator An animal that catches and kills other animals.

prey An animal that is caught and killed by a predator.

rainforests Dense forests found in tropical areas near the Equator.

red blood cells Cells that are part of the blood and carry oxygen, filled with haemoglobin.

reticulated Looking like a net or mesh.

savannah A grassland habitat with few trees found in tropical parts of Africa.

secrete To release a substance, for example, the skin cells of the poison frog secrete a poisonous substance.

sp. An abbreviation for 'species', used as part of the Latin name for animals where the exact species is unknown.

sperm Male gamete, or sex cell.

streamlined Having a shape that moves easily through water.

sub-alpine The habitat that is found on mountain slopes, just below the tree line.

surface area The area of the outside surface of an object.

tadpole The larval stage in the life cycle of a frog or toad.

temperate A moderate climate that lacks extremes in temperature.

terrestrial Living on land.

territory A range or area claimed and defended by an animal.

torpor A state of inactivity.

toxic Harmful, poisonous.

tropical Parts of the world that lie either side of the Equator, which usually have a hot, wet climate.

ultraviolet radiation (UV) Invisible light that is part of sunlight. Most UV is absorbed by the Earth's atmosphere. Too much UV can be harmful.

vertebrate An animal that has a backbone, for example fish, amphibians, reptiles, birds and mammals.

webbed feet Having skin connecting the toes, which is helpful for swimming.

FURTHER INFORMATION

Books

100 Things You Should Know About: Amphibians by Jinny Johnson (Miles Kelly Publishing, 2004)

21st Century Debates: Endangered Species by Malcolm Penny (Hodder Wayland, 2003)

Animal Classification by Polly Goodman (Hodder Wayland, 2004)

Animal Kingdom: Amphibians by Sally Morgan (Raintree, 2004)

Classifying Living Things: Classifying Amphibians by Andrew Solway (Heinemann Library, 2003)

DK Animal Encyclopedia (Dorling Kindersley, 2000)

The Encyclopedia of Animals: Mammals, Birds, Reptiles, Amphibians editors Forshaw, Gould and McKay (Fog City Press, 2002)

Life Processes series: *Classification* by Holly Wallace (Heinemann Library, 2002)

Nature Files series: *Animal Groupings* by Anita Ganeri (Heinemann Library, 2003)

Science Answers: Classification by Richard & Louise A. Spilsbury (Heinemann Library, 2004)

Visual Encyclopedia of Animals by Barbara Taylor (Dorling Kindersley, 2000)

Websites

All About Frogs
http://allaboutfrogs.org/
A website with facts, news items and stories about frogs.

Enchanted Learning
http://www.enchantedlearning.com/coloring/amphibians.shtml
Fact sheets, quizzes and drawings of many different amphibians.

Frog Web
http://frogweb.nbii.gov/index.html
A website with information about the decline of amphibians in North America and the appearance of malformed limbs. Includes species identification guides.

Frogs
http://www.exploratorium.edu/frogs/index.html
Website based on an exhibition that was run at the Exploratorium, San Francisco, USA. Plenty of frog articles, interactive exhibits and hands-on activities.

Yahooligans! Animals
http://yahooligans.yahoo.com/content/animals/amphibians/
Fact sheets on a range of amphibian species, as well as information about amphibian classification, defence and diet.

INDEX

Page numbers in bold refer to a photograph or illustration.